Mol
Guide Dog

Written by Barrie Wade
Photographed by Robert Pickett

Collins Educational
An imprint of HarperCollins*Publishers*

Molly guides her owner.

Molly stops at
the kerb.

Molly waits.
Her owner listens.

Molly crosses
when it is safe.

Molly goes into
the shop.

Molly goes into
the library.

Molly goes home
on the bus.